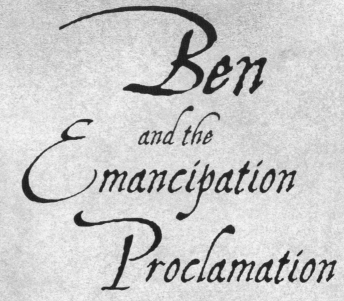

Ben
and the
Emancipation
Proclamation

Written by **Pat Sherman**

Illustrated by **Floyd Cooper**

Eerdmans Books for Young Readers

Grand Rapids, Michigan • Cambridge, U.K.

Text © 2010 Pat Sherman
Illustrations © 2010 Floyd Cooper

Published in 2010 by Eerdmans Books for Young Readers
an imprint of Wm. B. Eerdmans Publishing Co.

Wm. B. Eerdmans Publishing Co.
2140 Oak Industrial Dr. NE, Grand Rapids, Michigan 49505
P.O. Box 163, Cambridge CB3 9PU U.K.

www.eerdmans.com/youngreaders

Manufactured by Tien Wah Press in Singapore in September 2009, first printing

10 11 12 13 14 15 16   9 8 7 6 5 4 3 2 1

Library of Congress Cataloging-in-Publication Data

Sherman, Patrice.
Ben and the Emancipation Proclamation / by Patrice Sherman ; illustrated by Floyd Cooper.
p. cm.
ISBN 978-0-8028-5319-6 (alk. paper)
1. United States. President (1861-1865 : Lincoln). Emancipation Proclamation — Juvenile literature.
2. Slaves — Emancipation — United States — Juvenile literature. 3. Holmes, Benjamin C., fl. 1846-1870 — Juvenile literature.
I. Cooper, Floyd, ill. II. Title.
E453.S56 2010
973.7'14--dc22

2009026235

The illustrations were rendered in oil on board.
The display type was set in Aquiline.
The text type was set in Adobe Caslon Pro.

For my nephews Christopher, James, and Miles
— *P. S.*

For Beverly
— *F. C.*

"Excuse me, sir." Ben tugged on the sleeve of a passing gentleman. "Does that say Broad Street?" He pointed to the wooden sign on the corner.

"Yes." The man pulled away impatiently.

"And that other one, please. That's King Street, right?"

"Right."

Ben studied the signs, trying to remember the letters. Broad. B-R-O-A-D. King. K-I . . .

"Boy?" The man had turned to stare at him. "Shouldn't you be getting along?"

"Yes, sir." Ben threw his carrying sack over his shoulder and hurried away. *Don't let them know you can read.* That's what his father had told him. Slaves weren't allowed to read.

Ben's father had known how to read a little —
just enough to teach Ben the alphabet. But then
his father had been sold and now no one knew
where he was. Ben's mother had wanted him to
keep learning, but she couldn't read, and Ben
was so busy helping in the kitchen. He had no
time for alphabet letters.

A few months ago, though, the master
had apprenticed him to Mr. Bleeker, a tailor in
Charleston. Ben was still a slave, but he could
learn a trade and live in the city.

Learning the tailor trade wasn't easy.
Mr. Bleeker was always barking orders. Not
just "Dust the shelves!" or "Sweep the floor!"
but "Get me the extra-fine silk thread!" or
"Where did I put my ledger again?" Ben
wondered how Mr. Bleeker had ever found
anything before he came along. Ben spent
so much time searching and fetching, he
felt dizzy by the end of the day.

Then he discovered something wonderful. There were all kinds of secret ways to learn how to read. Almost without thinking, Ben had begun to recognize the names Mr. Bleeker wrote in the ledger. He could even tell what was inside the boxes on the shelves by the words on the outside.

"I don't know what it is about Ben," he heard Mr. Bleeker boast to a customer. "He just seems to know so much."

Now Mr. Bleeker was sending Ben on errands all over the city.

M-A-R-K-E-T. He turned onto Market Street. He loved walking around Charleston. There were words everywhere, on the sides of wagons and in store windows: Ice and Coal, Fresh Eggs and Cream, Hats and Gloves, China Teas.

S-T-A-T-I-O-N-E-R-Y. He studied the window. The stationery store sold paper, ink, and pens of all sorts.

Simon's Dry Goods Store, his next stop, was always busy. Ben studied the words on the shelves and barrels while he waited in line.

When his turn came, he handed Mrs. Bleeker's list to the girl behind the counter. Ben watched as she took things from the shelves.

"Uh, excuse me," Ben said pointing to the soap. "Mrs. Bleeker wants Pear's Soap, not Pearl's."

"That's Pear's." The girl slapped the box down hard.

"I mean, she said the kind that comes in the yellow box, not the blue one," Ben added quickly.

The clerk replaced the soap. Her face was sour.

"Well, you tell Miz Bleeker Pearl's Soap is as good as Pear's any day. See?"

"Yes, Ma'am." Ben piled everything into his sack, making sure it was all there. Mrs. Bleeker trusted him. Nothing was ever missing from her list.

Outside the store, Ben spied a copy of the *Charleston Mercury* that someone had tossed into the gutter. He snatched up the newspaper, glad to see that it wasn't too torn and dirty. He began to fold it into a hat as he walked along. Lots of boys and men, white and black, wore paper hats to keep off the sun. No one would wonder why he had a newspaper as long as he kept it on his head.

Before Ben got back to the tailor shop, he stopped beneath a big beech tree. The dense, low branches hid him from prying eyes as he unfolded the newspaper and spread it on the ground. He began searching for the names and words he had heard people talking about. Henry Clay . . . Daniel Webster . . . Abolition. A-B-O-L-I-T-I-O-N. Ben spelled it out. That word meant the end of slavery. Emancipation. E-M-A-N-C-I-P-A-T-I-O-N. That meant freedom. The *Charleston Mercury* didn't like those two words at all.

It was getting late. Ben rolled up the rest of the paper and stuffed it into his shirt.

After Ben had worked as an apprentice for a year, Mr. Bleeker gave him permission to visit his mother. He was allowed to spend a Sunday on the plantation, as long as he was back before sunset.

Ben was so excited he couldn't sleep. He got dressed in the dark, tucked a copy of the *Mercury* inside his shirt, and started the twelve-mile hike well before sunrise. If he hurried, Ben figured he'd be there by breakfast. The road wound past the tobacco fields where the field hands were already out working. No Sunday rest for them.

Word that Ben was coming got to the house before he did. His mother was waiting for him at the door. And everybody on the plantation who had family in Charleston wanted to see Ben. All morning, they asked him questions about their families and gave him messages to take back.

Finally, Ben and his mother had some time alone. First, Ben read her a passage from an old, worn Bible she had hidden in her room. Then he read her the newspaper, every word. She made him repeat the name "Abraham Lincoln" twice. "That's the new fellow that's running the country," Ben explained.

"I know," she said quietly. Ben noticed the tiredness in her voice. She had taken extra jobs, she told him, mending and sewing for ladies on nearby plantations, often working late into the night after her own chores were done. Slaves could earn extra money that way, penny by penny.

She reached into her apron pocket and took out a gold coin. She held it up. "This is a dollar." Ben had never seen a gold dollar before, not even in the tailor shop.

"When you learn to write, it will be yours," she said.

Ben began to study harder than ever. He wouldn't disappoint his mother.

When he swept the shop in the early morning, Ben wrote letters with his finger in the dust. When he washed the windows, he wrote letters with soap and quickly wiped them clean. He saved every scrap of paper Mr. Bleeker threw out and filled an empty ink well with water to make a pale ink. Then he whittled a twig to a sharp point and began to make letters on the back of the used paper.

The one thing he couldn't do was keep his reading and writing a secret from the other slaves. Word got around.

When he made deliveries, people pulled him into the kitchen or the little back rooms where they slept. "Teach us," they whispered.

"Teach me." The little girl scrubbing the steps asked him to write her name in water on the stones.

"Teach me." The boy shoveling coal wanted to write his name with soot.

"Teach me." Every place he went.

At Christmas, Ben's mother gave him the gold coin.

He never saw his mother again.

In the spring, war broke out between the states, and you didn't need a newspaper to know it. Overnight, the streets filled with soldiers in gray uniforms. A dozen times a day someone would stop Ben to ask where he was going. Over and over he repeated that he was Mr. Bleeker's boy, Ben, just running errands. He kept his eyes down. He didn't look at signs anymore.

But he still picked up a newspaper every chance he got.

As the Union Army pushed closer to the city, white people began to flee. The Bleekers boarded up their tailor shop. They had to go, Mr. Bleeker said. He was sorry they couldn't take Ben with them.

Ben was sent to a slave prison, the place where slaves had to stay until they were sold. The prison was a single large shed on the waterfront, so packed with men and boys that there was hardly any place to sit.

Weeks went by. No one knew what was going to happen. Some men insisted they were all going to be sold inland. Others claimed there was a whole regiment of black soldiers fighting for the Union up at Fort Wagner. They said they'd join up the minute they got the chance to run away.

Somebody even said that Lincoln had issued a Proclamation of Emancipation — that he had freed the slaves. Could Lincoln really do that? everyone asked.

Even though Ben wanted a newspaper more than anything, he kept quiet. He would just forget about reading. It could only lead to trouble.

One night someone jostled him awake. A voice whispered that the men had pooled all their bits of chewing tobacco together and bribed one of the guards for the latest copy of the *Mercury.*

They lit a torch so he could see. Ben squinted at the paper.

"Go on," someone murmured. "Read it. We all know you can read."

Ben hesitated.

"Read." Voices rose from the darkness. "Read!"

"The Message of Abraham Lincoln is to be found in this journal this morning . . ." Ben read softly.

"Louder," someone called out. "Stand up."

Slowly Ben stood up. Every man in the prison was awake, every face turned towards him. He drew a deep breath.

"On the first day of January, in the year of our Lord one thousand eight hundred and sixty-three . . ." His voice became stronger and clearer. "All persons held as slaves within any State or designated part of a State, the people whereof shall then be in rebellion against the United States, shall be then, thenceforward, and forever free. . . ."

Everyone broke into cheers. They stomped and clapped and didn't care who heard. After a moment, Ben realized they weren't just cheering for Abraham Lincoln; they were cheering for him too. For the first time in their lives, these men had heard a black man read out loud. Hands reached out to shake his. Talk swirled around him. What did this new freedom mean?

Ben reached into his pocket and touched his mother's gold coin. He knew she would have been proud of the way he read tonight.

Daylight was coming now. Ben peered through a chink between the slats of the shed. Whatever this new freedom looked like, he wanted to be the first to see it. Carefully, he folded up the newspaper and tucked it in his shirt, ready to read it again whenever he could.

Author's Note

Benjamin C. Holmes was born a slave in South Carolina in 1846 or 1848. His father, who had a little education, taught him a few letters of the alphabet. While still a child, Holmes was apprenticed to a tailor in Charleston. There, he taught himself to read by studying the signs on streets and in shop windows.

After the Civil War broke out, his master sent him to the slave prison in Charleston to await sale. While there, a copy of the *Charleston Mercury* was smuggled in and Holmes read the Emancipation Proclamation to the applause of his fellow inmates — certainly one of the most remarkable readings of that document ever recorded.

Like most slaves, he did not immediately gain his freedom. He was sent to Chattanooga, Tennessee, where he worked in a general store, eventually running the business when his new master was drafted into the Confederate Army. After the war he worked in several other businesses, but his main ambition in life remained education. In 1868 he enrolled in Nashville's newly founded Fisk University. An excellent singer, he was soon invited to join the school's chorus, which later became known as the Jubilee Singers. He toured with the Singers throughout America and Europe. He also taught in a rural school in Tennessee, a task he considered even more important than singing.

He died, probably of tuberculosis, in the early 1870s. The exact date of his death, like that of his birth, remains unknown.

Additional Sources on Benjamin Holmes and His World

BOOKS ———

Slave Spirituals and the Jubilee Singers, by Michael L. Cooper. New York: Clarion Books, 2001. A history of the Jubilee Singers and their music.

A Band of Angels: A Story Inspired by the Jubilee Singers, by Deborah Hopkinson; illustrated by Raúl Colón. New York: Atheneum Books for Young Readers, 1999. A biographical story based on the life of Ella Sheppard, one of the first Jubilee Singers.

Chariot in the Sky: A Story of the Jubilee Singers, by Arna Bontemps; illustrations by Cyrus Leroy Baldridge. Philadelphia: Winston, 1951; republished by Oxford University Press Children's Books, 2002. A novel based on Benjamin Holmes's life.

The Civil War Extra: From the Pages of the **Charleston Mercury** *&* **the** **New York Times**, edited by Eugene P. Moehring and Arleen Keylin. New York: Arno Press, 1975. This book contains many articles that Benjamin Holmes may have actually read.

WEBSITES ———
The Emancipation Proclamation
www.archives.gov/exhibits/featured_documents/emancipation_proclamation/

Fisk University
www.fisk.edu/page.asp?id=115

The Jubilee Singers: Sacrifice and Glory
www.pbs.org/wgbh/amex/singers/filmmore/index.html

The South Carolina Information Highway
www.sciway.net/afam/slavery/indexs.html